UPENDRA NATH RATH

BEYOND THE YEARS

The Life of Upendra Nath Rath

This is a work of nonfiction. The events and the incidents mentioned in the book are true and real. However, some names and characteristics have been changed, some events have been compressed, and some dialogues have been recreated.

First Edition: January 2026
Printed in India

Printed at: Thomson Press, New Delhi

Typeset in Cambria

ISBN: 978-93-6070-260-1

Cover Design: Prajakta Sawant

STORYMIRROR
Stories that reflect you

Publisher: StoryMirror Infotech Pvt. Ltd.
Unit No-F/705, 7th Floor, Kailas Corporate Lounge,
Veer Savarkar Road, Vikhroli Park Site,
Vikhroli West, Mumbai-400079,
Maharashtra, India.

Web: storymirror.com
Facebook: @storymirror
Twitter: @story_mirror
Instagram: @storymirror
Email: marketing@storymirror.com

The Life and Legacy of Upendra Nath Rath

International Writer · Poet · Social Reformer · Educator · Scout Veteran

DEDICATION

To my beloved parents, teachers, mentors,
students, and the countless souls whose love,
encouragement, and guidance shaped
the journey of my life.

TABLE OF CONTENTS

Preface 9

Acknowledgment 11

Autobiography

1. Childhood and Early Memories 15
2. High School Years 21
3. College Life and B.Ed. 27
4. Life at Lumding 31
5. The Waltair Years 33
6. Gopalpur — A New Beginning 35
7. Air Force Schools and Leadership 39
8. INS Chilika — Harmony in Service 41
9. Return to Gopalpur 43
10. Recognition and Awards 45
11. Final Posting at Berhampur 47
12. Life After Retirement 49

Achievements & Books

13. Achievements and Awards 53

14. Books by Upendra Nath Rath 55

15. International Writer's Journey 57

Poems & Reflections

16. Selected Poems 61

17. Reflections of Wisdom 111

18. Quotations 115

Closing

19. Final Reflection 123

20. Legacy Statement 125

Epilogue 127

PREFACE

I am extremely delighted to present this book in its present form, made possible by the divine blessings of Lord Jagannath, the Creator of the Universe. His grace has been the guiding force in turning this dream into reality.

I extend my heartfelt gratitude to my wife, Mrs. Pranati Mishra; my son, Er. Sandip Sanam Rath, a Software Engineer; and my daughter-in-law, Er. Samiksha Satapathy, also a Software Engineer, for their constant encouragement and motivating words that helped me shape this book.

A special mention goes to my beloved granddaughter, Shrishti Rath, whose innocent gestures and loving presence have added a unique charm to this work. Her delightful childhood activities inspire many of the reflections and quotations included here. I am sincerely thankful to my nephew Er. Asish Mishra for his editing, graphing, and designing.

This book also draws upon real-life experiences, which I sincerely hope will serve as a guiding light for readers across the globe.

I am deeply thankful to my friends, relatives, and well-wishers for their continuous support and encouragement throughout this journey.

My sincere gratitude to Story Mirror for their friendly cooperation and unwavering support in bringing this book to life.

Above all, I remain eternally grateful to my Mother, whose unwavering love and strength have always been with me in both joy and sorrow.

With warm regards,

Upendra Nath Rath

August 2025, International Writer, Poet and Story Writer

ACKNOWLEDGMENT

With deep humility and gratitude, I bow before Lord Jagannath, Supreme God, whose divine blessings and eternal presence have been my guiding light throughout the journey of my life and the making of this autobiography.

I express my heartfelt thanks to my beloved parents, teachers, mentors, colleagues, friends, and students, who shaped my thoughts, enriched my experiences, and supported me with unwavering encouragement. Their wisdom, affection, and guidance have left indelible marks upon my soul.

I remain grateful to the Scouting fraternity, literary circles, social reformers, and well-wishers across the globe, whose companionship and inspiration motivated me to dedicate myself to the cause of humanity, education, peace, and service. My heartfelt thanks to Balamukunda Pattnaik of Dura for type writing the whole book of Autobiography.

My sincere appreciation also goes to the publishers, Storymirror editors, and readers, who have encouraged me to bring forth my life story in its complete essence. Without their kind cooperation and patience, this book would not have reached its present form.

Above all, I acknowledge the love and support of my family members, whose sacrifices, understanding, and affection have been the foundation of my strength and determination.

This book is not only my personal journey but also a humble offering to society, literature, and future generations, with the hope that it may inspire, guide, and uplift all who turn its pages.

With profound regards

Upendra Nath Rath

International Writer and Poet

AUTOBIOGRAPHY

CHAPTER 1

CHILDHOOD AND EARLY MEMORIES

I was born into a modest, middle-class family in **Narasinghpur,** a small town in the Cuttack district of Odisha. The day was Chaturdashi, one day before the full moon in the month of **Magh**. My arrival brought joy to my family, but also many stories that shaped my early identity.

As a toddler, I started walking late. My grandmother lovingly called me "Chhota" in Odia, which literally meant "lame". But my father smiled and told me that Chhota was the name of a landlord who used to visit our village. He was admired by both children and adults, and by calling me Chhota, people wished to see the same charm in me.

At the age of three, while brushing my teeth with a neem twig, I fell, and the stick pierced my cheek. I was rushed to **Narasinghpur Hospital** where I spent three days under treatment before fully recovering. That incident left me with a scar — not just on my face, but also in my memory.

First Schooling

My early schooling began in **Kusanga,** now part of Boudh District in Odisha. Childhood there was filled with playfulness and curiosity. I often spent my time observing the beauty of nature — the moonlight, the green fields, and the playful birds.

When my father was transferred back to his native district of Cuttack, we lived in Kakhadi, near Athgarh Subdivision.

I remember my father's stories vividly. Once, on his way to Kusanga U.P. School, he narrowly escaped an elephant. Another man ignored his warning and challenged the elephant. Tragically, the elephant caught him with its trunk and threw him violently, ending his life. That story etched in me the lesson that courage must always be guided by wisdom.

Festivals and Adventures

During Dussehra Durga Puja, the OSRTC buses of Odisha were decorated like brides and adorned with flowers, and children were given free rides. Those childhood festivals filled me with wonder.

At four years old, I learned swimming in the village pond *Solabandha.* Once, during the rainy season, a **myna bird** fell into the pond. While my friends only watched, I jumped in and swam to rescue the helpless bird. I carried it gently to the bank. My father, though relieved, slapped me for risking my life. That day I learned a profound lesson: **saving a life brings joy, but courage must be balanced with caution.**

The Magic Show and First Lessons

At the age of five, I was asked to go to the weekly village market, which was held on Tuesdays and Fridays. That day also happened to be the day of my Class I examination at Solabandha Primary School.

At the market, I was captivated by a magic show. Hours passed until I suddenly remembered the examination. I rushed back home, got ready, and ran to school. To my relief, the headmaster announced the exam was cancelled due to bad weather. I silently thanked God.

In school, discipline was strict. Teachers would send students to search for absentees hiding in the fields. Once, I found classmates hiding under straw heaps and brought them back. That was the era when **teachers took responsibility for shaping character, not just teaching lessons.**

Middle School Days

After passing Class V, I was admitted to **Champeswar M.E. School** in Class VI. Sitting on benches and desks for the first time felt like a great joy.

In English class, our teacher Shri Banamali Sarangi once asked a boy, Bharat, to spell the word "car". Bharat mischievously said mor (meaning "mine" in Odia). The whole class laughed, but the teacher punished him. It was a reminder that learning is serious, yet joy and mistakes are part of the journey.

In Class VII, my SST teacher Shri Gadadhar Mahalik told me: *"Upendra, you are a fortunate boy. Your broad forehead shows that one day you will achieve greatness."* His words remain engraved in my heart. A poem is written to dedicate in his loving memory.

In Champeswar school, so calm, so bright,
We learned by day, we dreamed by night.
With books and pens, with soil and seeds,
We grew in knowledge, fulfilled our needs.

We watered plants with tender care,
Fenced with branches, work to share.
At harvest time, so fair, so sweet,
The fruits of labor made life complete.

One part for school, one kept for grain,
One shared with students, joy to gain.
Our teachers guided, true and kind,
They shaped our hearts, they trained our mind.

Among them stood, with gentle grace,
Shri Mahalik, a shining face.
He taught us lessons, deep and clear,
With patient love, he drew us near.

One day he called me, soft and true,
"Upendra, greatness waits for you.
Upon your brow, I see the light,
You'll spread your name both far and bright."

His words still echo, strong and pure,
A blessing eternal, a vision sure.
His prophecy bloomed, his love my guide,
I bow to my Guru with grateful pride.

We were also given small plots of land in school to grow onions, radishes, and turnips during craft classes. My friend **Purna Chandra Jani** and I cultivated radishes so big that they became the centre of attraction. Together we fenced the plots with thorny branches from *Dali Changudi* mountain. It was hard work, but it taught us the dignity of labour and the beauty of teamwork.

CHAPTER 2

HIGH SCHOOL YEARS

The Encounter with a Bear

One Saturday, while collecting thorny branches from **Dali Changudi Mountain** for our school garden, I discovered a bear snoring inside a cave. Mischievously, I threw a small stone to see what would happen. To my horror, the bear charged out. My friends and I ran down the slope at full speed, our hearts racing. We escaped unharmed. That day I thanked God for saving me and promised myself to channel my curiosity with wisdom.

Festivals in School

Our Headmaster at Champeswar M.E. School, **Anand Chandra Panda,** was a kind and inspiring man. He taught English and encouraged us to organize festivals and feasts, especially during **Saraswati Puja** and **Ganesh Puja.**

Every student brought rice or dal from home. A small contribution was collected for vegetables. Teachers and students cooked together, and we sat side by side, sharing food with joy. These celebrations taught us that **education is not only about books, but also about togetherness, culture, and values.**

Entry into High School

When I entered **Champeswar Gram Panchayat High School,** life became more demanding. Students from many surrounding villages came to study here.

Our PET (Physical Education Teacher), **Shri Debaraj Sahoo**, was a good athlete who also taught Odia. He organized sports events where I competed in the slow-cycle race and won **3rd prize.** I still preserve the certificate as a token of memory.

Lessons in Science

One of the most inspiring teachers was **Shri Purna Chandra Panda,** our science teacher. He was disciplined, dedicated, and passionate. He performed experiments with hydrogen and oxygen gases, and even showed us how soap could be made using caustic soda and oil. The sparkle in his eyes while teaching made science come alive. His lessons remain etched in my memory.

Later, **Shri Durga Madhab Mishra** joined as an assistant teacher. During his interview, he explained a poem by Gopal Krushna Patnaik with such clarity and depth that the entire panel and students were mesmerized. He was appointed immediately. He never punished students harshly, and his calm, disciplined nature earned everyone's respect.

The Essay on Women's Education

One day in Class X, our English teacher asked us to write an essay on women's education. I wrote it beautifully, including the word luxury. The teacher asked me the meaning of the word in class. Though I knew, I stayed silent. He asked another student to fetch a cane and struck me several times. I felt humiliated, but I did not argue. That day I realized a truth: **a teacher must study child psychology, and children deserve respect both at home and in school.**

Grammar Lessons with the Headmaster

Our Headmaster, **Shri Prafulla Chandra. Panda,** taught English grammar every Saturday. His explanations of grammar rules were clear, logical, and inspiring. I still remember many of those rules decades later, which helped me throughout my writing journey.

Friendships that Lasted

High school was not only about teachers and books. It was about friendship. Friends like

Niranjan Nayak, Pradyumna Sarangi, Biren Kumar Mohapatra, Fakir Nayak, Magiram Muduli, Biranch Narayan Sahoo, Bhabagrahi Ghadei, Gita Panda, and Kanak made school life vibrant. We shared food during recess, exchanged fruits, and supported each other through challenges.

Mischief in Sanskrit Class

Our Sanskrit teacher, **Shri Hare Krushna Satapathy,** was strict yet caring. One day, I brought a large insect (sunari) tied with a thread and kept it in my pocket. Suddenly it crawled out during class, buzzing loudly. The entire class laughed. When I admitted my mischief, I was punished. That incident transformed me into a disciplined student. I realized that **fun has its place, but responsibility must guide actions.**

Risky Adventures in the Village

Apart from studies, we often engaged in small adventures in the village. Sometimes, we organized picnics or roasted pigeon peas in straw fires.

Once, three of us — me, Pradyumna Sarangi, and Niranjan Nayak — went to collect pigeon peas from a well-known area called Balikua (sand well). It was a dark winter evening. As we reached the spot, we heard the terrifying hiss of a poisonous snake. Terrified, we ran in different directions until we reached the safety of the village. That night we breathed a sigh of relief and promised never to repeat such dangerous mischief.

Preparing for the Board Examination

In Class X, the focus shifted to preparing for the board exams. Friends bought **OSTA Test Papers,** while I purchased **Modern Bharati Test Papers.** We revised together, discussed questions, and supported one another. Our teachers wished us success, reminding us that **hard work and faith always bring results.**

When the board results were declared, I passed with confidence and was selected for admission to **Government College, Sundargarh.**

First Step into College Life

Sundargarh Government College was a beautiful institution, located on the outskirts of the city. For the first time, I experienced a little ragging. Once, a small misunderstanding with a student named Paresh from Balangir almost led to conflict. But when I explained myself to Dibya Shankar Singhdeo, one of the senior students, the matter was amicably resolved. Later, Dibya became one of my good friends.

At college, I admired P**rofessor G. Ranga Rao**, a versatile genius in English literature. His teaching was clear and captivating. I also respected **Shri Susil Kumar Topno**, who taught Political Science with great depth. Through him, I learned about **Plato, Aristotle, Machiavelli, Hobbes, Locke, and Rousseau** — lessons that continue to influence my reflections today.

CHAPTER 3

COLLEGE LIFE AND THE ROAD TO TEACHING

College Years in Sundargarh

My years at Government College, Sundargarh were transformative. Beyond academics, college life opened new windows to friendships, challenges, and personal growth.

In the second year, our college faced a long spell of student agitation. Classes were suspended for months. Many students missed their tests and even skipped the final examination, thinking it was a heroic act of protest. But I believed education was sacred. I persevered, appeared for the exams, and when results were declared, I passed with Second Class Honours.

The Path to B.Ed.

After completing my B.A., I decided to pursue **Bachelor of Education (B.Ed.)** in Sundargarh.

The college was new, filled with fresh energy, and buzzing with aspirations. Our lecturer, **Shri Sevak Tripathy**, explained lessons with such clarity that our doubts would melt away.

Many students came from places like Chaibasa and Shadeikala. They stayed in modest rented houses near the colony. Once I visited my friends **Sunil** and **Dipachand** and was amazed at their cooking technique — they cooked rice, dal, and eggs together in a single pot, cleverly separating the items in cloth pouches. It was not only practical but also an inspiring lesson in **resourcefulness and economy.**

Student Union Elections

During my B.Ed. year, student union elections were held. Many friends encouraged me to contest for the post of President, but I humbly filed my nomination for **Cultural Secretary.** To my surprise and delight, I was elected.

One of our memorable activities was a picnic to **Khandadhar Waterfall.** We sang, danced, and prepared meals together amidst the breathtaking beauty of nature. The cold mist from the falls refreshed us even in summer. On our return journey, we stopped at a roadside eatery. Though there were no meals, we satisfied our hunger with boiled potatoes. The trip remains etched in my memory as a symbol of **joy, friendship, and simplicity.**

My First Appointment as Headmaster

After my B.Ed., I was fortunate to be appointed as **Headmaster at Sidhamula High School**, later known as *Gokulananda Jew Bidyamandir.*

The school was more than a workplace — it was a mission. Local leaders like **Shri Prabhakar Mishra, Kashinath Swain, Sarthak Mahalik, and Surya Narayan Rath** worked tirelessly for the development of both the school and the village. My colleagues, including **Bharat Pradhan and Pradyumna Sarangi,** were devoted to teaching. Together, we taught classes, mentored students, and guided the community with sincerity.

Some of my students stayed with me in the school premises. They were bright, obedient, and hungry for knowledge. Among them were **Bira Bara Sahoo, Mayadhar Nayak, Kalandi Behera, and Katlia Sethi.** I tutored them personally, ensuring they received not only education but also values for life.

A Life in the Village

Sidhamula was a place of warmth and togetherness. My close friend **Madhusudan Mishra,** a retired army man, treated me like family. He often invited me for feasts at his home, and even gifted me a **Hercules bicyclc** which I used for my daily commute. His generosity and companionship remain unforgettable.

It was Madhusudan who once advised me to purchase land in Gania. His words proved wise, and later he himself settled there. To this day, we remain connected by phone and memory.

The Leap to Kendriya Vidyalaya

One day, my brother Rama Chandra Mishra suggested:

"Upendra, why don't you apply for a teaching post in Kendriya Vidyalaya Sangathan?"

Encouraged, I applied. To my joy, I was selected and posted to **Kendriya Vidyalaya, Lumding,** a railway junction town. This was the beginning of a long and meaningful journey with Kendriya Vidyalayas across India.

CHAPTER 4

LIFE AT LUMDING

First Impressions

At Lumding, I was allotted a small **railway quarter** near the tracks. The rumbling of engines at night initially made sleep impossible. But soon, I adapted.

My neighbours were teachers from Bihar. Their family seemed kind, but an incident taught me caution. One day, their elderly father offered me a large bowl of curd. Something felt odd, so I poured it away. Later, he admitted a rat had fallen into the bowl. I silently thanked God for guiding me away from danger.

Bonds of Friendship

At Lumding, I made several lifelong friends. **Shri Manik Chakraborty,** a junior clerk, was a man of music and athletics. He often invited me to lunch at his home. I also befriended **Ram Kirti Yelaw, Khirod Chandra Boro, Pariram Brahona, Sucheta Choudhury, and Anjana Dutta.**

Our Principal, Shri R.Y. Rai, was a storyteller who loved to share anecdotes from his previous postings. During his absence, I was given the responsibility as Acting Principal — my first taste of leadership in Kendriya Vidyalaya.

Service to Others

Once, my colleague **Anjana Dutta**, a music teacher, returned home to find her entire house robbed. She was devastated. Knowing I had rapport with railway and police authorities, she sought my help. I approached the RPSF (Railway Protection Security Force) commandant, Shri Sengar, whose son was my student. He acted promptly. Within days, stolen items were recovered and returned. Anjana expressed her heartfelt gratitude.

Such moments strengthened my belief that **a teacher's duty goes beyond classrooms; it is service to humanity.**

Travels and Cultural Lessons

During vacations, my friend **Rajib Lochan Nayak** and I often travelled to Berhampur by train. Lumding also gave me glimpses of diverse cultures. When I visited Nagaland, I saw markets where bargaining was unheard of. People bought goods at the price quoted by shopkeepers. It was an entirely new world of values and practices.

CHAPTER 5

THE WALTAIR YEARS

Transfer to Visakhapatnam (Waltair)

After a few enriching years in Lumding, I was transferred to **Kendriya Vidyalaya, Waltair,** in Visakhapatnam. The bustling city, with its serene beaches and hills, offered a striking contrast to the quiet railway colony life of Lumding.

At Waltair, I worked under inspiring leaders and soon found myself entrusted with responsibilities beyond classroom teaching. I frequently visited the nearby **K.V. Steel Plant** to interact in academic and cultural activities.

It was here that I forged a lifelong friendship with **Shri Bhagaban Nayak,** whose sons **Papun and Mithoon** were bright students. Our families shared many meals, conversations, and cultural outings.

Stronger Bonds with Students

Visakhapatnam students were talented and energetic. They eagerly participated in debates, poetry recitations, and cultural programs. I encouraged them to read widely and think critically. Many of them later became doctors, engineers, and officers. When they write to me today, expressing gratitude, I feel the noblest reward of my teaching career.

CHAPTER 6

GOPALPUR – A NEW BEGINNING

Opening a New School

In **July 1991**, I was transferred to the newly established **K.V. Gopalpur,** a military station near Berhampur. With **Shri L.K. Panda** as Principal and **G. Padhi** as my colleague, we were among the pioneers who shouldered the task of building the school from scratch.

There were no ready-made records, no organized admission systems, and no established cultural programs. Yet, with determination and teamwork, we laid the foundation of a vibrant institution. **Col. U.R. Mishra,** the nominee chairman, extended his coopcration and support.

Planting Seeds of Greenery

Beyond academics, I felt a duty to create a green learning environment. I collected saplings from

Berhampur University nursery, Chatrapur, and Digapahandi, often bearing the expenses myself. Soon, mango, guava, coconut, and shade trees transformed the barren campus into a lush garden of knowledge.

Students watered the plants daily. Many of those trees still stand tall today, a living testament to our efforts. I believe **teaching is not only about books; it is also about teaching children to nurture nature.**

Scout and Guide Leadership

At Gopalpur, I intensified my involvement in **Scouting and Guiding.** As a **Himalayn Wood Badge (HWB) Holder and Veteran Trainer,** I organized camps, community service, and rallies.

We trained students in self-reliance, discipline, and patriotism. I led service camps in villages like **Baxipalli, Golabandha, Digipur, and Berhampur,** distributing food, clothing, and moral support to the old and destitute. Scouts organized **vigilance awareness rallies** to fight corruption, **environmental drives** to spread green consciousness, and **blood donation camps** for humanitarian service.

Cultural Enrichment

Festivals and cultural events at K.V. Gopalpur became memorable occasions. Students staged **dramas, folk dances, and debates.** Once, I invited Chhau Nritya artists from Mayurbhanj to perform.

Their mesmerizing performance of *Abhimanyu Badh* left students and teachers spellbound.

These cultural activities were not just entertainment — they were lessons in **heritage, teamwork, and confidence.**

CHAPTER 7

THE JOURNEY TO AIR FORCE SCHOOLS

Surplus Teacher Transfer

In 1999, due to policy changes, one section was withdrawn and three teachers, including me, were declared surplus. I represented my case at KVS Headquarters, New Delhi. After due consideration, I was transferred to K.V. A.F.S. Salua.

Dedication at Salua

At Salua, I worked with colleagues **Mr. Binayak Chandra Bhat** and **Mr. Rabindra Kumar Martha,** both sincere and hardworking. In 1999, Mr. P. Shakthivel joined as Principal and transformed the school into one of the most competent in the Bhubaneswar Region.

I taught his children, Sundar and Gayatri, with special care. Mr. Shakthivel trusted me deeply, entrusting me with responsibilities such as furniture-in-charge, co-curricular activities in charge, and Scouts and Guides leadership. Together, we achieved 100% academic results, national recognition in cultural activities, and regional awards in Scouts.

CHAPTER 8

HARMONY IN SERVICE

New Assignment

In **2004**, I applied for a transfer closer to home and was posted to **K.V. INS Chilika,** inside the naval base. The serene environment of the lake blended beautifully with the discipline of the navy.

My colleagues included **Shri B. Nayak, Shri A.K. Padhi, Shri S. Padhi, and Shri Satyajit Mishra,** who commuted daily by train from Berhampur. Despite the distance, their dedication was inspiring.

Teaching Moments

One day, while teaching the lesson *"Yellow Butterfly",* a real yellow butterfly flew into the classroom. I gently caught it, showed it to the students, and released it. The class erupted with joy. Such coincidences felt like blessings, where **nature itself joined the classroom as a teacher.**

Lessons in Humility

During my walks to the railway station, I once saw five cows lying dead, victims of reckless driving. That tragic sight reminded me of the fragility of life and the urgent need for compassion towards animals.

Another time, while laughing at a group of monkeys near the mango trees, I realized they were about to attack. I stopped immediately and learned never to mock nature. Respecting every creature became a lifelong principle.

CHAPTER 9

RETURN TO GOPALPUR

A Second Innings

In **2006**, I was again posted to **K.V. Gopalpur Military Station,** where **Shri K.C. Nanda** was the Principal. He was punctual, disciplined, and began every morning assembly with a 20-minutes motivational address. His leadership inspired staff and students alike.

I continued my mission of **planting trees**. With my own resources, I brought saplings from Berhampur University nursery, Chatrapur, and Digapahandi. Slowly, the barren land bloomed into groves of mango, guava, and shade trees. Students enjoyed sitting beneath them, and the campus became a green oasis.

Leadership of Madam Biraja Mishra

After Shri Nanda retired in **2009, Mrs. Snehasuta Sadangi** took charge, followed by **Madam Biraja Mishra**, transferred from K.V. No. 3 Mancheswar.

Under her leadership, the school reached new heights:

100% board results in Class X.

Rajya Puraskar Scouts & Guides awards for many students.

A student received the **President's Award in Scouting.**

Recognition of teachers with **Incentive Awards**.

During her tenure, I was awarded a **Medal of Merit** for my contributions. These moments reaffirmed my belief that sincere teamwork always yields excellence.

Cultural Excellence

With Madam Mishra's encouragement, I organized a **Chhau Nritya performance** of *Abhimanyu Badh* by artists from Mayurbhanj district. The rhythmic drums, vibrant costumes, and heroic tale left an indelible mark on the students.

We also held **plantation drives, health awareness rallies, and inter-school workshops** that brought recognition at both regional and national levels.

CHAPTER 10

RECOGNITION AND AWARDS

Incentive Award 2014

In 2014, I was deeply honoured to receive an Incentive Award from Deputy Commissioner R. Kalavati of the Bhubaneswar Region. The citation recognised my decades of service in:

Scouting and Guiding.

Green initiatives and environmental education.

Cultural enrichment in schools.

Educational excellence.

The award ceremony was not just a personal achievement, but a tribute to all the students, colleagues, and well-wishers who had been part of my journey.

International Recognition

In later years, my work as a writer, poet, and social reformer brought international recognition. Among these, the letter of appreciation for his excellency from President of Switzerland for promoting peace was a crowning moment.

These honors reaffirmed my lifelong belief:

"Service with sincerity, teaching with love, and writing with wisdom are the true paths to immortality."

CHAPTER 11

FINAL POSTING AT BERHAMPUR

The Berhampur Chapter

In **2019**, I was transferred to **K.V. Berhampur,** where **Shri Bighneswar Patnaik** was the Principal.

He welcomed me warmly and quickly became not only a colleague but also a trusted friend. His administrative skills were sharp; his discipline firm yet always delivered with a smile. Together, we organized:

Workshops for teachers.

Scout camps.

Rajya and Rashtrapati Puraskar examinations, where I served as observer and examiner.

Shri Patnaik's work ethic was inspiring — he worked tirelessly from dawn till late at night. Our relationship extended beyond school; he became like family.

Superannuation in 2022

On **31 May 2022,** I retired after decades of dedicated service in Kendriya Vidyalayas. The Vidyalaya organized a **grand farewell function.** Students performed cultural programs, colleagues spoke with affection, and a warm reception was followed by a feast.

When I finally left the campus, Principal **Shri Patnaik,** Headmaster **H. Panda,** and colleague **Ghadei** personally accompanied me home. Their gesture filled my heart with gratitude.

CHAPTER 12

LIFE AFTER RETIREMENT

A New Rhythm of Life

Retirement was not an end, but a **new beginning.** My days now begin at 5:30 a.m. with a **3 km walk** and **respiratory exercises.** I pluck flowers for puja, chant slokas of Shiva, Hanumanji, and Gayatri, and maintain a **vegetarian lifestyle.**

I spend time in my garden where I grow chickoo, guava, coconut, spinach, mustard, and onions. **The chickoo** tree from Gate Bazaar, Kharagpur, began bearing fruit after four years, yielding thrice a year. The fruits are sweet and shared with friends.

Companions in Nature

Every morning, two **crows** visit my mango tree, waiting for biscuits. A **white cat** comes daily for milk and bread. Street dogs **Kalia and his mate** leap with joy whenever they see me. I used to watch the activities of mongoose at back side of my house daily. Some of them peeped at me in a happy and delightful gesture.

Such bonds with animals remind me that **love transcends species.**

Time for Writing and Reflection

Now, I dedicate my mornings to reading newspapers, replying to emails, and working on **books, poems, and reflections**. Writing has become not only my passion but my spiritual duty.

Through my books such as *Spectrum of Indian Heritage and Reflections of Wisdom,* I continue to reach readers across India and abroad, spreading values of peace, ethics, and humanity.

ACHIEVEMENTS & BOOKS

CHAPTER 13

ACHIEVEMENTS AND AWARDS

National Service through Education

My career as a teacher and Headmaster across Kendriya Vidyalayas spanned four decades. Each posting brought new challenges, but also opportunities to make an impact. My key achievements include:

100% pass rate in Class X at multiple schools.

Establishing **newly opened Kendriya Vidyalayas** (Lumding, Gopalpur, Srikakulam.)

Organizing **service camps** for the destitute and victims of slum fires.

Leading **Scouting and Guiding initiatives,** training thousands of students in discipline, service, and patriotism.

Planting **hundreds of trees** across campuses, transforming barren grounds into green sanctuaries.

Recognitions within Kendriya Vidyalaya Sangathan

Medal of Merit — awarded for dedication to Scouting, social service, and student welfare.

Incentive Award — by Deputy Commissioner R. Kalavati, recognizing my role in academic excellence, environmental initiatives, and co-curricular achievements.

Rajya Puraskar and Rashtrapati Puraskar — many of my students received these prestigious awards in Scouts and Guides under my mentorship.

International Recognition

My contributions as a writer and poet carried my voice beyond the boundaries of India. Among the honors, the most memorable include:

Letter of Appreciation from his Excellency, President Switzerland for Promoting World Peace.

Acknowledgment as an International Writer and Poet whose reflections on ethics, culture, society, and humanity have been published worldwide.

Invitations from **literary forums and cultural organizations abroad** to share thoughts on peace, heritage, and universal values.

These honours reaffirmed my conviction that **literature has the power to cross borders, unite hearts, and inspire generations.**

CHAPTER 14

BOOKS BY UPENDRA NATH RATH

Spectrum of Indian Heritage

Published by **24/7 Publication, Kolkata,** this book is a celebration of India's rich culture, traditions, and values. It reflects upon the wisdom embedded in our history, folklore, festivals, and philosophy. Through its pages, readers are taken on a journey into the **soul of Indian civilization.**

Reflections of Wisdom

This book is a collection of inspiring thoughts drawn from **nature, society, ethics, culture, history, geography, education, political science, and psychology.**

Its quotations emphasize the eternal values of:

Skilful speaking and positive influence.

Silence as a source of inner peace.

The contrast between material wealth and true knowledge.

The omnipresence of God in human life.

Every page carries a thought meant to **inspire, enlighten, and guide.** Many of these reflections are now quoted by students, educators, and readers across India and abroad.

Poetry Collections

As a **poet**, I have written extensively on themes of:

Nature: birds, trees, rivers, the changing seasons.

Spirituality: devotion to God, reflections on silence, and faith.

Patriotism: poems on national unity, martyrs, and India's eternal heritage.

Human values: kindness, discipline, courage, honesty, and service.

My poems are known for their **rhythm, simplicity, and moral depth,** written to touch not just the mind but also the soul.

CHAPTER 15

INTERNATIONAL WRITER JOURNEY

From Odisha to the World

What began in the small town of Narasinghpur eventually found its voice across the globe. My poems and essays have been published in **national newspapers and international journals.**

I have contributed to leading publications such as:

The Indian Express

The Times of India

The Samaj

Anupam Bharat

Each article or poem carried a message of **social reform, peace, and ethical responsibility.**

A Columnist and Social Reformer

My columns often addressed:

The need for **environmental consciousness.**

Ethics in education and employment.

The role of **youth in shaping society.**

The importance of **peaceful coexistence in a diverse world.**

These writings became my way of engaging with society — **not just as a teacher, but as a reformer and motivator.**

Literary Themes and Vision

Across my writings, a few themes remain constant:

Peace is the highest pursuit of humanity.

Knowledge outweighs material wealth.

Silence, humility, and service are the roots of wisdom.

All religions lead to the same ocean of truth.

It is these reflections that have given my work its **universal appeal,** earning me the reputation of an **International Writer and Poet.**

Beyond Awards and Recognition

While awards are gratifying, the **smiles of students, gratitude of villagers, and blessings of elders** remain my true achievements.

As I reflect on my journey, I realize that every award, every book, and every poem is a humble offering to God, society, and humanity.

POEMS & REFLECTIONS

CHAPTER 16

SELECTED POEMS

1: Start Your Day with Joy

Start your day with a happy beginning,
Thank God for life and each blessing.
Pray for a world so wondrous and bright,
Filled with miracles, love, and light.
Walk a while, let your body be free,
Exercise gently, beneath the tree.
Watch the birds in colors untold,
Feed the hungry, young and old.
Help the orphan, the sick, the weak,
Do your duty with love unique.
Serve your nation with heart sincere,
Safeguard its treasures year by year.

Green your locality, spread delight,
Work with courage, choose the right.

Thus each morning will clearly showthat the seeds of greatness in you will grow.

2: National Unity

India, my nation, diverse and vast,
With heritage deep and culture steadfast.
From Kashmir's peaks to Kanyakumari's shore,
Unity and strength forevermore.
Languages many, yet voices unite,
Customs and colors in harmony bright.
Our dresses, dances, foods, and song,
Form a tapestry where all belong.
No storm can break this sacred chain,
No power can divide this golden plain.
Together we stand, together we rise,
India shines beneath the skies.

3: Song of Eternity

India, an icon of eternity,
Source of wisdom and unity.
Its flame of truth forever burns,
And through the ages the whole world learns.
From Vedas' chants to Buddha's call,
Compassion flows to one and all.
Saints and sages, brave and wise,
Gave us lessons time still applies to.
O Motherland, your soul is vast,
A bridge from future to the past.
Eternal beacon, bright and free,
Guide the world to harmony.

4: Song of the Unsung Martyrs

Across the world, in lands afar,
Lie heroes unknown, each a star.
Their names unsung, their deeds profound,
In silence deep, their glories sound.
Some fought for freedom, some for peace,
Their struggles sought the world's release.
No trumpet hailed, no banner flew,
Yet history owes its light to few.
We sing today their noble fight,
They lit the world with truth and light.
O martyrs brave, though unsung, unseen,
Your sacrifice keeps our nation clean.

5: The Sound of the Crow

At dawn the crow cries loud and clear,
“Awake, O world, a new day is near!”
By noon it caws with steady tone,
“Do your duty, the time is your own.”
At dusk it calls with plain wisdom,
“Rest, O soul, you’ve much to gain.”
Though a simple bird, of blackened hue,
Its voice recalls what’s good and true.
O humble crow, your sound may be a hidden guide for humanity.
Through day and night, your message flows,
a timeless rhythm the cosmos knows.

6: Life is a Journey

Life is a journey, winding and long,
A path of trials, yet filled with song.
Not always straight, but curved with care,
Of joy and sorrow, a balanced share.
Ups and downs, both night and day,
Guide our steps along the way.
Yet we move forward, strong and wise,
Chasing hope beneath the skies.
Be positive — life's truest art,
Negativity breaks the human heart.
Together we walk, through dark and sun,
Till brighter dawns for all are won.

7: Be Brave and Courageous

Life is a laboratory, full of tests,
Some are easy, some are complex.
Truth and falsehood, joy and strife,
Mark the pattern of human life.
Be brave, be steadfast, never bend,
For trials and storms will always end.
Clouds will vanish; light will appear,
The dawn of freedom will soon be near.
Slavery to freedom, night to day,
Innovation lights the noblest way.
Be courageous, hold on tight,
With faith and hope, the world grows bright.

8: A Happy Beginning

Start your day with a cheerful heart,
Thank God for blessings, a brand-new start.
Pray for a world both wondrous and bright,
Full of miracles, beauty, and light.

Move your body with exercise fair,
Walk with strength, breathe fresh air.
Admire the colors of birds in flight,
Feed the creatures, spread delight.

Offer your hand to the weak and in pain,
To orphans, the needy — ease their strain.
Work with integrity, honest and true,
Give your best in all you do.

Protect the nation, its treasures hold dear,
Support the government, be sincere.
Join society's noble cause,
Abide by justice, respect the laws.

Plant more trees, let greenery grow,
Make your locality bloom and glow.
A day well started with kindness and grace,
Will spread happiness in every place.

9: Epic Of The Divine Hand

In the quiet hymn of morning,
When sunrays kissed the earth,
I journeyed forth to Berhampur—
A path of simple worth.
The hour struck half past nine,
The breeze was soft and cool,
And I, with mind in perfect peace,
Rode forth as calm as any pool.

Before the gate of AADC,
Where the little pond lies still,
Where washermen cleanse the garments old
By nature's gentle will—
There destiny unfolded
A tale unseen, untold,
A battle between man and fate,
And faith both brave and bold.

My Scooty, steady till that point,
Began its fateful slide—
A sudden pull towards the left,
A drift no hand could guide.
Alert I was, awake to all,
My senses sharp and clear—
Yet brakes obeyed no mortal wish,
No force could interfere.

Towards the edge it dragged me on,
Beyond my human might,
Where three feet down the earth sloped low
In shadow, stone, and light.
The world above grew distant
As I tumbled with the fall,
Among the jagged rocks that stood
Like guardians old and tall.

My helmet clasped my temples tight—
A soldier in that war,
Shielding me from nature's rage
And every hidden scar.
Silence wrapped its mantle round,
No footsteps met my cry;
I called to passing travellers,
But none turned ear or eye.

Alone, yet not abandoned,
I felt a force unseen—
A whisper in the void of fear,
A presence calm, serene.
Strength rose like sudden sunrise
In the chambers of my chest,
And I, who lay forsaken,
Stood once more, blessed.

With effort born of spirit,
I raised the fallen steel,
Pushed it back to road and light
By Heaven's silent zeal.
And lo! my flesh was spotless—
No bruise, no cut, no trail—
A miracle unquestioned,
Where mortal senses fail.

I thanked the Supreme Spirit,
The Keeper of the day,
Who guards the honest-hearted
Upon their righteous way.
For God walks not in thunder,
Nor in tempests fierce and loud—
He walks with those whose hearts are true,
Unseen among the crowd.

I journeyed on to Berhampur,
Completed every task,
Returned in peace, returned in joy—
A grace no man can ask.
And thus I learned a lesson
That life and fate impart:
Good souls, sincere in duty,
Carry God within their heart.

When wicked souls may wander,
When selfish minds betray,
A pure and faithful spirit
Shall never lose its way.
For when the world is silent,
And helpers disappear,
The Eternal One stands closest—
His whisper conquers fear.

Believe in Him, O traveller—
Walk truthfully, walk strong;
For God protects the selfless path
And rights the hidden wrong.
When human hands abandon,
When shadows close around,
The Divine Hand lifts the fallen soul
And places it on sacred ground.

So let this tale be witness—
A testament of grace,
That faith can move the unseen realm
And time cannot erase.
For blessed are those who labour
With honest heart and mind,
For God Himself walks by their side—
The Guardian of mankind.

9: My Mother

Once, as usual, I began my day with my simple daily routine. I went to the nearby market at Karapalli, close to my home, and purchased a few daily essentials—vegetables, fruits, and household items. After returning home and completing my breakfast, I started my journey to Berhampur, nearly fifteen kilometres away.

On the way stands the famous deity Maa Maradiamma, deeply revered across our locality. People from all walks of life visit her sacred place to offer prayers, perform rituals, and express gratitude when their wishes are fulfilled. Many feasts and spiritual ceremonies are organised throughout the year. My devotion to Maa has always been profound, and her temple holds a special place in my life.

As I reached the temple that day, I noticed a tall, slim lady sitting quietly under a tree. She wore a saree, and the sindoor on her forehead glowed in the sunlight. After offering my prayers, I heard her call out to me:

"Beta, come here. I am very hungry. Give me some food."

I replied gently, "Mother, please wait. I will bring something from the nearby stall." But she insisted softly:

"The Goddess's Prasad is here. Give it to me."

For a moment, I hesitated. Then, remembering the boundless compassion and power of Maa Maradiamma, I offered her the Prasad with a silent prayer. She ate it with deep contentment and asked for water. I immediately went on my scooter, bought a bottle of water, and handed it to her. With heartfelt gratitude, she blessed me and mentioned she was going on a tirth yatra (pilgrimage). She asked if I could give her some money.

Whatever amount I had with me, I offered wholeheartedly. She accepted it joyfully. But a little later, when I looked back, she had completely vanished. Nowhere to be seen.

It was miraculous. Surprising. Unbelievable. Yet entirely true. Such divine encounters grace a person's life only rarely.

Many years earlier, around that time, my own mother had been admitted to SUN Hospital by my brother. Initially, the doctor had said her condition was stable, so I returned home. Suddenly, a call came—her condition had worsened, and an urgent operation was required. By the time I reached, the surgery was over. She lay on the bed, speaking in an unclear voice, struggling.

The next day... she left this earthly world. I could not witness her last breath. That pain—of not being there—remained with me for days, months, and years.

But after encountering the mysterious Mother at the feet of Maa Maradiamma, an immense peace swept over me. A realization dawned:

> My mother had come to bless me. A mother is eternal—forever, across all lifetimes.

11: The Miracle of a Dream

Dreams are dreams — so strange, so bright,
Some fade at dawn, some glow at night.
Some ring true with a golden gleam,
Some dissolve — a fleeting dream.

Some bring lessons, deep and wise,
Some bring tears to waking eyes.
Some are charming, warm, and fair,
Some bring gloom we cannot bear.

Each day's moment, joy or pain,
Echoes softly in the brain.
Woven threads of thought remain,
Flowing down the mind's deep lane.

From conscious shore to hidden stream,
The heart gives birth to every dream.
From subconscious fields they rise,
Painting truth beneath disguise.

At twenty-one, my heart did gleam,
I dreamt a pure, prophetic dream.
A postman came — his step so light,
A brown envelope in morning light.

My father called, "Sanei, come here,
What message shines so bright and clear?"
He read aloud — oh joy untold!
"An appointment letter," pure as gold!

"Upendra's chosen," the postman said,
And cheers of bliss around us spread.
In humble home, with hearts agleam,
We felt the miracle of dream.

Dreams are not mere shades of night,
They hold a spark, divine and bright.
For faith and hope in souls redeem —
Life itself is born from dream.

Life itself is born from dream...

12: True Happiness Lies in Simplicity and Togetherness

Some individuals believe that living in a grand, luxurious mansion, dining on expensive food, or wearing branded clothes will bring them ultimate happiness and pleasure. But this belief is as wrong as wrong can be.

True happiness blossoms when one becomes sociable, amicable, and treats everyone equally without discrimination. One should learn to adjust gracefully with every situation — only then can real joy be experienced.

Love your people, your culture, your food, and your environment — and you will discover the true essence of happiness.

13: Eternal Tribute to Upendra Nath Rath.

O name that shines with noble grace,
A guiding star for time and space;
Upendra Nath Rath, the world does sing,
A poet, a leader, a true Scout king.

International writer, voice of light,
Your words awaken hearts at night;
Through poems and prose, your spirit flows,
A fountain of peace where wisdom grows.

A veteran Scout with service rare,
You build a world beyond despair;
Teaching the young, inspiring all,
To rise with courage, to heed the call.

Protector of forests, of rivers and seas,
Guardian of sparrows, of flowers and trees;
An environmentalist, steadfast, strong,
Restoring the Earth where all belong.

Forefront leader of cleansing hands,
You sow pure hope in towns and lands;
A brand of peace the globe adorns,
A herald of love where light is born.

Beloved of people, of skies and streams,
Bearer of visions, of radiant dreams;
Your heart embraces both great and small,
A servant of truth, a friend to all.

O Rath, whose soul the world admires,
Whose steps ignite celestial fires;
May every dawn proclaim your name,
An eternal torch, an undying flame.

14: Glory of Shiva – A Poetic Tribute

No words can tell, no mind can see,
The boundless Lord of eternity.
Beyond the stars, beyond the skies,
Shiva the Great, the Supreme, the Wise.

Brahma creates, and Vishnu sustains,
But Shiva's power in all remains.
The source, the end, the cosmic flame,
All worlds exist within His name.

With ash He shines, so pure, so bright,
Detached from wealth, from worldly might.
Snakes as jewels, the Ganga flows,
Upon His locks divinity glows.

The cosmic dance, His wondrous art,
Creation's beat, destruction's start.
Through every step the heavens sing,
He is the timeless, deathless King.

Compassion vast, His gift so free,
To humble souls on bended knee.
Not grandeur wins His boundless grace,
But love that flows from heart's embrace.

O Shiva Shankar, ever true,
The hymn of Pushpadanta grew.
Yet still Your greatness none can bind,
You dwell beyond both space and mind.

So may we praise, with voices small,
The Lord who shelters one and all.
In Him lies peace, in Him release,
In Him the soul finds endless bliss.
Upendra Nath Rath, International Writer, Poet and Story Writer.

15: Guardians of the Earth

The morning sun, the skies so bright,
The moon that glows with gentle light.
The rivers sing, the oceans call,
The Earth is home, the heart of all.

The forests deep, the fields so green,
The beauty vast, the sights serene.
The songs of birds, the buzzing bees,
The whispers soft of dancing trees.

If we protect, the Earth will thrive,
Its breath will keep our dreams alive.
But if we harm, the cost we'll pay,
The joy of life may fade away.

So hand in hand, let's make a vow,
To love the Earth, protect it now.
For future's sake, for you and me,
We are the Earth,
And Earth is we.
Upendra Nath Rath, International Writer,
Poet and Story Writer.

16: Jai Ganesh, Remover of Hurdles

Ganesh, the first of Gods adored,
With trunk so curved, by all implored.
Son of Parvati, Shiva's might,
He blesses all with wisdom's light.

In Kailas high, Lord Shiva said,
"No soul shall pass, no step shall tread."
Ganesh stood firm at duty's call,
Guarding his mother, dearest of all.

The guards opposed, a struggle grew,
Ganesh resisted, bold and true.
Shiva in anger, fierce and wild,
Struck down the mother's precious child.

Parvati wept in deep despair,
Her lifeless son lay fallen there.
Shiva repented, Gods all came,
To give new life, restore his name.

Brahma spoke wise: "An elephant's head,
Placed on the child, shall wake the dead."
The deed was done, the boy arose,
Blessed by all, as story shows.

"First among Gods you'll ever be,
Remover of hurdles, eternally.
Granting wealth, and wisdom bright,
Strength and virtue, love and light."

So hearts resound in joyous strain:
"Jai Jai Ganesh, forever reign!
Jai Jai Ganesh, remover of pain!
Jai Jai Ganesh, our hope, our gain!"
Upendra Nath Rath International Writer ,Poet and
Story Writer

17: Waves of Life

Life flows like a mighty stream,
Carrying hopes, carrying dream.
With sunlit dawns and stormy skies,
New lessons bloom, old sorrow dies.

Each step we take, a story told,
Of burning trials and hearts so bold.
In pain we learn, in joy we grow,
Through darkest nights, our spirits glow.

The world's a stage, yet none can bind,
The freedom soaring in the mind.
With love as lamp and truth as guide,
We sail through tempests, far and wide.

Oh waves of life, both rough and kind,
You shape the soul, you clear the mind.
And in your flow, I find my art,
An endless song from heart to heart.

17: Rise with Determination

With steadfast will and heart so true,
Life opens doors with dreams anew.
Through work and ethics, pure devotion,
Dedication fuels the ocean.

No clock can bind the soul's own flight,
Each path is carved by inner light.
Respect the mind, both strong and kind,
For treasure lies in toil refined.

Labour sincere will never decay,
Hope will guide the weary way.
Pray to God with humble grace,
Serve the needy, lift their face.

Love the birds, the plants, the trees,
Embrace the world with gentle ease.
Speak golden words, let kindness flow,
In daily life let virtues grow.

One day you'll see, with vision clear,
A blessed change is drawing near.
For God bestows what hearts can be—
A life of strength, of harmony.

Upendra Nath Rath
International Writer and Poet

18: Body,Mind and Soul

The body is the temple, strong and true,
It works each day in all we do.
Hands that labor, feet that tread,
A living form where life is spread.

The mind's a lantern, bright and wise,
It shapes our thoughts, it lifts the skies.
Dreams and ideas in silence bloom,
It clears the path, removes the gloom.

The soul's a flame, eternal, divine,
A guiding star that makes us shine.
It sings of truth, of peace, of love,
Connecting earth to heaven above.

When body, mind, and soul unite,
Life becomes a beam of light.
With harmony, we reach the whole,
The trinity makes a perfect soul.

18: Children and School Days

Childhood shines, a golden ray,
A treasure of life, that fades away.
With books and play, with laugh and fun,
A journey of joy for everyone.

Reading lessons, making cheer,
Whispers of mischief, teachers hear.
Picnics bright, and trips so grand,
Memories bloom like grains of sand.

Scouting calls with spirit high,
Under the vast and open sky.
Running, jumping, games to play,
Volleyball, Kabaddi, make the day.

Slow cycle rides, with laughter near,
NCC pride, with hearts sincere.
Hands that serve when troubles flow,
Helping the needy in flood's deep woe.

Cyclones pass, yet children stand,
With courage strong, they lend a hand.
Content and pure, their hearts remain,
Such school-time bliss won't come again.

19: Our Changing Food

From childhood days we learn to eat,
Simple meals, so fresh, so sweet.
Rice,pulses, curry fruits so fair,
Nature's gifts beyond compare.

But when wealth begins to grow,
Fashioned tastes begin to show.
Pizza, burger, noodles too,
Take the place of what we knew.

Such foods bring style, but not much gain,
They gift us trouble, ache, and pain.
Constipation, poisoning, strife,
They slowly spoil the joy of life.

So let us keep the habits old,
The meals of health, pure and bold.
For healthy food makes mind refined,
A shining body, a peaceful mind.
Upendra Nath Rath, International Writer and Poet

20: Joy of Giving

The joy of giving shines so bright,
A noble deed, a sacred light.
It lifts the soul, it warms the heart,
Of love and service, it is a part.

Not all will walk this selfless way,
But blessed ones find joy each day.
They give their time, their care, their hand,
To heal the wounds across the land.

In flood, in fire, in cyclone's roar,
They rush to help, they give much more.
Though they may suffer, hunger too,
They ease the pain of others in view.

For giving brings a gentle peace,
A joy within that will not cease.
God smiles upon the hearts so kind,
Who serve with love, with soul refined.

Upendra Nath Rath, International Writer and Poet

21: The Song of Harappa

In valleys where the rivers flowed,
A mighty, hidden city glowed.
With bricks of fire, so strong, so true,
They built a world both old and new.

The streets were straight, the drains ran deep,
Their wisdom woke while others sleep.
The Great Bath stood in noble pride,
Where ritual waters purified.

The farmers sowed their golden grain,
They traded beads across the plain.
To distant lands their goods would sail,
Through Mesopotamian trail.

The artisans with gentle hands,
Made seals and toys in many lands.
With silver, copper, beads that shine,
Their crafts were truly so divine.

Yet time would turn, the rivers change,
The cities fell, the end seemed strange.
But still their story lives today,
In ruins where their echoes stay.

O Harappa, O Mohenjo's lore,
Your voice shall sing forevermore.
A tale of culture, strength, and art,
That shaped the world right from the start.
Upendra Nath Rath
International Writer and Poet.

22: Present Scene

In this age of glitter, shallow and bright,
False glamour shines more than honest light.
Voices loud with hollow claim,
Yet true skill hides without a name.

Those with little, pretend to know all,
While silent masters watch pride fall.
Duplicity thrives, corruption wears a crown,
The noble and wise are beaten down.

Continental halls with feasts so wide,
The corrupted dine with boastful pride.
The hungry toil, with sweat and pain,
Yet their hard labour goes in vain.

Students honest, with sleepless nights,
Find doors closed despite their rights.
While cheats with paper, forged and sly,
Step ahead as others cry.

Toppers who once wore laurel's crest,
Now take bribes, betraying the test.
Marks are gifted, bought with gold,
While truth is silenced, left untold.

The noble soul bears heavier chains,
The honest heart suffers endless pains.
Leaders stay silent, justice delayed,
Protests rise but soon they fade.

Yet hope still whispers through the storm,
That better times will once transform.
Peace shall reign, truth will prevail,
Falsehood and greed at last shall fail.

With noble hands and righteous sway,
A golden dawn will light the way.
Justice shall bloom, corruption undone,
And Rama Rajya will surely return.
Upendra Nath Rath
International Writer & Poet

23: Song of Peace

Peace shall blossom, bright and true,
In every heart, both old and new.
Good souls with noble, tender heart,
Will light the world and play their part.

With selfless love, with tireless hand,
They heal the earth, they guide the land.
Through labour hard, through friendship deep,
The seeds of hope the just will reap.

Cooperation, courage strong,
Shall turn the pain to joyous song.
Though falsehood tries, it cannot stay,
For truth shall shine and lead the way.

Justice will reign, the chains shall fall,
Peace will embrace and bless us all.
Together we'll rise, together we'll sing,
A brighter dawn the world shall bring.

Upendra Nath Rath
International Writer & Poet

24: My father,my pride

My father working under British reign
Working as Cashier and counting countless coins
Collects and bring coins from one place to another
He was the sole incharge of the full bags coin
Never found deceived to them Hilzer company
Who was assigned to collect taxes
Had my father misused the money,He would have enjoyed his life with pleasure and gain
He never adopted unfair means
Through his honesty,in last part of life ,he suffered some time.
Still be never broke down
Honest not made him prominent yetI am blessed as him worthy Son.
(In the loving memory of My father late Bidyadhar Rath)

25: God sees the truth but Waits

God sees the truth, though hidden deep,

No secret lies His eyes can keep.
The wicked shine for but a day,
Their borrowed light will fade away.

The honest heart may suffer long,
The weak be crushed, oppressed by strong.
Yet Heaven waits, in silence still,
To test the soul, to shape the will.

Though justice walks with patient stride,
It cannot fail, it will not hide.
The lies shall fall, the masks shall break,
The truth shall rise for all men's sake.

So bear with courage, calm and bright,
Through darkest hour, through longest night.
For God delays—but not in vain,
His truth shall heal all human pain.
Upendra Nath Rath
International Writer & Poet

26: Symphony of Nature

The river flows with silver gleam,
Whispering songs, a timeless dream.
It meets the sea with arms so wide,
Where waves embrace the rushing tide.

The meadows bloom in tender green,
With dancing grass, a living sheen.
The mountains rise, both vast and tall,
The valleys echo nature's call.

Sunshine spills its golden rays,
On children's laughter, carefree plays.
Birds are singing in skies so blue,
The cuckoo calls with music true.

Trees bear fruits, both sweet and bright,
A gift of earth, a pure delight.
Happiness reigns, the heart beats free,
In nature's arms, eternity.

Oh joy that flows in every part,
From sky above to human heart.
This world's a hymn, serene and fair,
God's gentle love is everywhere.

Upendra Nath Rath
International Writer & Poet

27: Beauty of Nature

In abundance shines the morning light,
The sun ascends with golden might.
The meadows laugh in emerald hue,
A boundless glory, fresh and new.

Mango groves with fragrance sweet,
Offer shade from noonday heat.
A pond reflects the sky so wide,
Where lilies bloom and ripples glide.

Cows are grazing, calm and free,
Cornfields sway like waves at sea.
A farmer tills with patient hand,
Bringing life to fertile land.

By shaded trees, young minds engage,
Students study, page by page.
Knowledge grows, like seeds that rise,
A harvest bright beneath the skies.

Women dance in graceful flow,
Their joy like rivers, pure they show.
Drums resound, the voices sing,
A hymn of life to God they bring.

O Nature vast, O sacred story,
Your beauty tells of God's own glory.
From dawn till dusk, both near and far,
You shine His light, a guiding star.
Upendra Nath Rath, International Writer, Poet and Story Writer.

28: Infant and Computer in Modern Technology

An infant smiles with eyes so bright,
Unfolding dreams in tender light.
Beside him hums the screen's soft glow,
A modern world he soon will know.

Tiny fingers reach and play,
While gadgets guide the minds today.
From toys to tablets, tools appear,
Shaping futures, far and near.

Yet let the child still hear the song,
Of nature's birds that sing along.
For modern wonders, vast and deep,
Must guard the soul that dreams in sleep.

A balance true the world must find,
Where heart and code in peace are twined.
So infant hope and tech combine,
To build tomorrow's grand design.
Upendra Nath Rath International Writer ,Poet and Story Writer

29: Study Tour to Kanha National Park

Our study tour to Kanha began,
With eager hearts and a joyful plan.
Through forest paths, so deep and green,
Nature's wonders we had seen.

Deer and rabbits crossed our way,
Peacocks danced in bright array.
In Maruti gypsies we rode with cheer,
Hoping the tiger would soon appear.

Footprints told of the tiger's might,
We followed the trail with keen delight.
On elephant's back, so high, so strong,
We moved through the jungle's song.

By the stream a tiger lay,
Calmly resting in the day.
We watched in awe, so close, so near,
Yet felt no danger, only cheer.

The forest officer, wise and kind,
Shared his thoughts to shape our mind:
"In Kanha, tigers roam at will,
But cause no harm, they mean no ill."

Our study tour gave lessons grand,
Of nature's gifts across the land.
Kanha's glory we shall recall,
A treasure of learning, shared by all.
Upendra Nath Rath
International Writer,Poet and Story Writer

30: Chilka – A Glory of Nature, Land and Sky

On a study tour we made our way,
To Chilka's charm at break of day.
By bus we traveled, hearts so light,
With laughter and joy, our spirits bright.

At OTDC Hotel we took our breakfast
Then boarded a boat with fervent zeal.
The lake lay vast, serene, and wide,
Its waves a mirror of heaven's pride.

Birds of colors, red, green, and blue,
Chirping sweet songs as they swiftly flew.
Boats like paintings, a wondrous sight,
Glistening sun spread golden light.

Hundreds of boats moved to and fro,
On gentle waters with rhythmic flow.
Sudden delight our eyes did meet,
Dolphins dancing—graceful, fleet.

We bowed before Kalijai divine,
Whose temple stands on waves' design.
Though time compelled our steps to part,
Chilka remained within each heart.

Birds, boats, dolphins, forest patrol,
Etched their beauty in mind and soul.
A glory of nature, beneath vast sky,
Chilka's memory shall never die.

Upendra Nath Rath
International Writer and Poet

31: World Peace, A Glorious Dream

The rivers whisper, the mountains pray,
That harmony shall rule the day.
Birds in chorus, the winds in flight,
Call mankind to choose the light.

Where silence speaks, no guns resound,
Only brotherhood on sacred ground.
The heart of man, so vast, so deep,
Must vows of peace forever keep.

Beyond all borders, caste, and creed,
Let love alone be human's deed.
No hatred's fire, no jealous art,
But friendship glowing in every heart.

From meadows green to oceans wide,
Let nations walk in equal stride.
As Rath has sung through noble lines,
Peace is the star that ever shines.

O children of earth, awake, arise,
Let kindness bloom beneath the skies.
For world peace prospers, pure, supreme delight.

Upendra Nath Rath International Writer, Poet and Story Writer

32: Pleasure of Reading

Reading's a joy, a treasure untold,
A lifelong companion, more precious than gold.
Learning continues, it never will cease,
It nurtures the mind, it blossoms with peace.

It widens horizons, both near and afar,
Extends our vision to life's every star.
Ideas take flight, new concepts are born,
Like rays of the sun on a radiant morn.

It builds up knowledge, both simple and deep,
Awakens the soul from ignorance sleep.
It shapes our lifestyle, it strengthens our way,
Guiding our footsteps by night and by day.

It draws us together, in wisdom we meet,
In reading's pure pleasure, our hearts find it sweet.
A process unending, a journey so true,
Reading brings joy, ever fresh, ever new.

Upendra Nath Rath, International Writer, Poet and Story Writer

33: Inner Satisfaction of Social Service

Service of others brings peace to the soul,
A passion eternal, a life-giving goal.
Not driven by fashion, nor forced by demand,
But guided by values, both noble and grand.

It's dignity shining, not weakness or shame,
An inner conviction, humanity's flame.
For causes of justice, for needs of the poor,
True service gives meaning, it opens the door.

Not for the earning, nor wealth to acquire,
But sharing and caring that lift and inspire.
To nourish the hungry, bring healing from pain,
To cleanse earth of toxins, of greed's heavy stain.

To free every mind from the darkness of night,
Through knowledge and learning, we welcome the light.
Awareness we spread—of health, of clean air,
Of saving our rivers, our forests so rare.

A world without hunger, with literacy's grace,
With harmony reigning in every place.
This is the mission, the pledge we embrace,
To serve all humanity, the whole human race.

Upendra Nath Rath
International Writer and Poet

CHAPTER 17

REFLECTIONS OF WISDOM

These reflections are drawn from my life, faith, and service. Each carries a message for humanity, shaped by ethics, culture, spirituality, and lived experience.

On Silence

Silence is the most powerful language.

It keeps peace within and prevents quarrels outside.

One who masters silence, masters life.

On Peace

Peace is not the absence of conflict,

but the presence of understanding.

A peaceful mind builds a peaceful society.

On Positive Influence

A skilful speaker can heal wounds,
inspire minds, and guide generations.
Words, when spoken with love,
become seeds of transformation.

On Wealth and Knowledge

Material wealth may build houses,
but true knowledge builds nations.
Riches vanish, but vision, wisdom and understanding
remain treasures forever.

On God's Presence

The Supreme God is omnipresent.
Nothing escapes His eye,
for He knows every detail of human life.
To live with this awareness is to live with truth.

On Nature

Every tree is a silent teacher,
every river a flowing lesson.
When we learn from nature,
we understand life more deeply.

On Honesty

Honesty is the highest ornament of character.
It may not bring instant success,
but it brings eternal respect.

On Courage

Courage is not the absence of fear,
but the ability to move forward despite fear.
History remembers the courageous,
not the fearful.

On Service

Service is the true prayer to God.
To serve the needy, the old, and the destitute
is to serve the Divine Himself.

On Education

Education is not only about passing exams.
It is the art of shaping life,
the discipline of mind, and
the awakening of soul.

On Friendship

True friendship is a bond of hearts,
not of convenience.

It is tested not in moments of joy,
but in the trials of life.

On Discipline

Discipline is the foundation of success.
It transforms dreams into achievements,
and chaos into harmony.

On Legacy

One may die,
but the legacy of values and good deeds
lives forever in the hearts of others.

On Leadership

A leader does not command. He inspires.
True leadership is service,
not power.

On Spirituality

All religions are like rivers,
flowing into the same ocean of truth.
Respecting every path
is the essence of spirituality.

CHAPTER 18

QUOTATIONS

On Education

Education is the light that removes the darkness of ignorance.

True education shapes not only the mind but also the character.

A teacher's smile can inspire more than a thousand lectures.

Discipline in education builds discipline in life.

Schools are temples where knowledge is worshipped and wisdom is born.

— Upendra Nath Rath

On Humanity

Humanity is greater than nationality, caste, or creed.

Service to humanity is service to God.

A kind heart can heal wounds that medicine cannot.

When you wipe a tear, you write poetry in the soul of God.

Humanity shines brightest when we care for the weakest.

— *Upendra Nath Rath*

On Peace

Peace begins with one calm heart and spreads to a thousand.

Weapons cannot bring peace; only wisdom can.

A peaceful world is built by peaceful minds.

Conflict divides; compassion unites.

The fragrance of peace is stronger than the fire of war.

— Upendra Nath Rath

On Leadership

A leader is not one who commands, but one who guides.

Leadership is service, not authority.

The best leader is the one who makes others believe in themselves.

A true leader listens more than he speaks.

Leadership is not a position — it is a responsibility.

— *Upendra Nath Rath*

On Courage and Optimism

Courage is the bridge between fear and achievement.

When darkness covers the sky, remember: the sun still shines above.

Hope is the seed from which courage grows.

Optimism is not ignoring reality; it is believing in possibility.

The storm tests the tree, but also strengthens its roots.

— Upendra Nath Rath

On Spirituality and God

God's presence is everywhere; His silence speaks louder than words.

All paths, though different, lead to the same Divine truth.

Prayer is not asking, it is connecting.

Silence in worship reveals God more than speeches in temples.

The heart that serves is closer to God than the lips that preach.

— *Upendra Nath Rath*

On Nature

A tree teaches patience more than any book.

Rivers remind us to move forward, no matter the obstacles.

The song of a bird is a hymn of gratitude to life.

Respect nature, for it is the first scripture of humanity.

In the silence of forests, the soul hears its own voice.

— *Upendra Nath Rath*

On Values and Character

Honesty is the key that unlocks trust.

Integrity is doing the right thing when no one is watching.

Character is not built in comfort, but in challenge.

A disciplined mind is a fortress against temptation.

Values are the roots; achievements are the fruits.

— *Upendra Nath Rath*

On Friendship and Love

Friendship is the art of sharing silence without discomfort.

True love is not possession, but protection.

Friends multiply joys and divide sorrows.

Love without respect is a flower without fragrance.

In the garden of life, friendship is the sweetest bloom.

— *Upendra Nath Rath*

On Legacy and Life

Life is short, but values make it eternal.

A man may die, but his deeds live forever.

The greatest wealth is the good we leave behind.

Life is a journey, not a race.

Write your story in kindness, so it may be read in eternity.

— *Upendra Nath Rath*

CLOSING

CHAPTER 19

FINAL REFLECTION

As I look back upon the journey of my life, from the small village of Narasinghpur to classrooms across India, from green plantations to international recognitions, I see one truth shining above all:

Life is valuable only when it is lived for others.

My humble beginnings taught me simplicity. My education gave me confidence. My career as a teacher gave me purpose. My writings gave me voice. And my service to society gave me peace.

I have walked through struggles and victories, faced failures and triumphs, and stood by faith in God throughout. If there is one message my life carries, it is this:

Be honest. Be courageous. Love nature. Serve humanity. And never stop learning.

CHAPTER 20

LEGACY STATEMENT

I do not measure success by wealth, property, or position. True success lies in:

The students who grew into responsible citizens.

The trees that still provide shade in the schools I nurtured.

The Scouts and Guides who became disciplined leaders.

The poems and reflections that continue to inspire readers.

The lives uplifted by service in villages and camps.

This, I believe, is my true legacy — a legacy of values, wisdom, and humanity.

When future generations read my books or recite my poems, may they not just admire the words, but also live the ideals behind them.

EPILOGUE

In the twilight of my years, I find joy in small things — the call of birds, the innocence of rabbits, the loyalty of street dogs, and the devotion of prayer.

I am grateful to my family, my friends, my students, and my readers. Each of them is part of my story. Each has contributed to the man I became.

If my life is remembered at all, let it be remembered not for awards or recognition, but for one simple truth:

I lived as a teacher, served as a reformer and writer, and wrote as a poet of humanity.

— *Upendra Nath Rath*

Upendra Nath Rath with International Connectivity

A Global Voice Rooted in Odisha

Born in the cultural heartland of Odisha, I began my writings with a strong sense of belonging to the soil, history, and traditions of India. Yet, from the very beginning, I believed that literature should not be confined within narrow borders. Words have wings; they must travel across landscapes, languages, and nations. My pen became my bridge to the world, and gradually, my voice found recognition in international literary and cultural spaces.

My Writings Beyond Borders

My books—Spectrum of Indian Heritage, Reflections of Wisdom, and my wide collection of poetry and essays—carry reflections not only on India's spiritual, historical, and cultural legacy but also on universal human concerns. They discuss ethics, peace, environment, and human psychology—subjects that resonate with readers globally.

In Switzerland, in America, in Europe, in the Middle East, and across Asia, I began to receive letters of appreciation from scholars, writers, and peace organizations. My reflections, deeply inspired by both Indian philosophy and global human values, became bridges of understanding. Literature became my passport to international connectivity.

Recognition Across Nations

It was a moment of pride when I was honored with the Letter of appreciation from President, Switzerland for Promoting World Peace. This recognition was not merely for my literary achievements but for my contribution to global peace and harmony. To me, this award symbolized the world acknowledging the message of compassion, duty, and truth that I have always upheld in my writings and social work.

I have been invited to share my views in international forums where peace, education, and cultural heritage are discussed. Each platform reaffirmed my belief that literature is the most powerful ambassador of humanity.

Literature as a Global Language

Poetry is not bound by geography. A reflection written in Odisha can touch a heart in London, New York, or Tokyo. When my poems were translated and circulated abroad, I realized the universality of human emotions. Whether it is the pain of poverty, the joy of spring, the silence of nature, or the eternal search for God—these are experiences every human soul shares.

In this way, my writings became part of an international dialogue on values. My essays on ethics, culture, and human psychology were welcomed not just as Indian perspectives but as contributions to the global treasury of wisdom.

The Humanitarian Dimension

My international connectivity is not limited to writing alone. Through Scouting and my social reform activities, I contributed to plantation programs, village service camps, and youth training camps. These initiatives carried messages of environmental consciousness and social responsibility that aligned with the United Nations' goals of sustainability and peace.

As a veteran scout trainer with the Himalyan Wood Badge (HWB), I interacted with leaders from other nations, exchanging ideas on how youth movements can shape a better future. This, too, became a channel of global connectivity—where the values of "Service, Duty, and Brotherhood" united young people across the world.

An Indian Voice for the World

Even as my works travelled internationally, I never detached myself from my roots. My international connectivity is grounded in my identity as an Indian writer, poet, and reformer. I believe that India's spiritual legacy has something vital to offer the world: the ideas of truth, non-violence, tolerance, and the eternal search for wisdom.

In my reflections, I have often contrasted the temporary glitter of material wealth with the everlasting power of knowledge, vision, and understanding. These are not only Indian values but also universal principles that can guide humanity.

Letters and Acknowledgments from Abroad

Over the years, I have received correspondence from readers and institutions abroad who found in my writings a voice of clarity and moral strength. Many told me that my reflections on silence, skillful speaking, and positive influence inspired them in their personal and professional lives. Others admired the way I combined history, politics, and ethics into life lessons.

Such acknowledgments reassured me that my words were not lost in the noise of the modern world; they were being heard, appreciated, and lived by people I had never met.

The Legacy of Global Connectivity

International connectivity is not just about recognition or awards; it is about responsibility. It places upon me the duty to continue writing with honesty, courage, and vision. When a writer's words travel across borders, they become part of the collective conscience of humanity.

My dream has always been to create not only a literary identity but also a human identity that bridges nations. In every reflection, I strive to remind readers that we are one human family—diverse in culture, yet united in our longing for peace and truth.

The World as One Family

Today, when I look back, I see my journey as proof of how a writer from Odisha can connect with the world. From the villages of my homeland to international forums of peace, from columns in Indian newspapers to acknowledgments abroad, my pen has carried me far beyond boundaries.

Thus, the phrase "Upendra Nath Rath with International Connectivity" is not only a description of my life but a testimony to the power of literature, service, and values to unite humanity.

Connectivity with Birds, Animals, Flora, Fauna, Rivers, Oceans, and Universal Truth

Living in Harmony with Nature

Since childhood, I have felt a deep spiritual connection with the natural world. The chirping of birds at dawn, the silent gaze of animals, the rustling of trees, and the flowing waters of rivers were not just sights and sounds for me—they were voices of wisdom. Nature became my greatest teacher, instilling in me lessons of patience, resilience, and universal truth.

Birds as Messengers of Freedom

Birds have always fascinated me. Their ability to soar freely in the sky symbolizes the unchained spirit of humanity. Watching a bird build its nest with care, feed its young with love, and sing at sunrise taught me that life must be lived with diligence, sacrifice, and joy. To me, birds are poets of the sky, whispering the eternal truth that freedom is both a gift and a responsibility.

Animals and the Language of Innocence

Animals, in their simplicity and innocence, reflect the purity of creation. Their loyalty, courage, and instinct reveal truths that often escape human society. A dog's devotion, a cow's gentleness, or a lion's strength shows that nature has designed every creature with purpose. I often saw in animals a mirror of human emotions, reminding me that compassion towards them is also compassion towards ourselves.

Flora and Fauna — The Garden of Life

The flora and fauna of our world form the great garden of life. Each tree, flower, and herb is a page in God's book of creation. During my planting drives in schools and villages, I realized that planting a tree is not merely an act of greenery—it is planting hope, shelter, and life for generations to come.

The fragrance of a flower, the shade of a banyan tree, the medicinal value of herbs—these are the silent gifts of nature. Respecting flora and fauna is respecting the cycle of life.

Rivers — The Eternal Flow

Rivers are sacred to me. They carry the stories of civilizations, the blessings of rain, and the eternal message of continuity. Watching a river flow reminded me that life, too, must move forward despite obstacles. A river nourishes fields, quenches thirst, and finally merges with the ocean, just as a human life nourishes society and finally merges with the Universal Spirit.

Oceans — The Depth of Mystery

The ocean, vast and infinite, has always awakened a sense of awe in me. Its waves speak of power, while its depths conceal mysteries unknown. To stand by the shore is to understand humility: no matter how great we are, the universe is greater. The ocean teaches patience, strength, and the truth that beneath every surface lies unseen depth.

Universal Truth through Nature

My connection with birds, animals, rivers, and oceans ultimately leads me to the universal truth: that all forms of life are interconnected. Humanity is not the master of nature but a humble participant in its cycle. The sun rises for all, the river flows for all, the tree gives shade to all—so must our lives be lived in service to all.

Nature constantly whispers lessons:

From birds: freedom and responsibility.

From animals: loyalty, innocence, and strength.

From flora and fauna: beauty, healing, and balance.

From rivers: continuity and purpose.

From oceans: depth, mystery, and humility.

Together, they point to the eternal truth that life is One, and the Creator dwells in every leaf, every wing, every drop, and every heartbeat.

One with Creation

In my journey as a writer and reformer, I have always carried these lessons. My poetry, reflections, and social work are rooted in this deep connection with nature. Just as a river connects villages and an ocean connects continents, so too does my life strive to connect humanity with the universal truth of peace, love, and harmony.

Thus, Upendra Nath Rath's connection with birds, animals, flora, fauna, rivers, and oceans is not only ecological but spiritual—a bridge leading to the eternal truth that binds all creation as one family.

OTHER BOOK BY THE AUTHOR:

Memorable Quotations - Part - 1 (2nd Edition):
https://amzn.in/d/gfCcrym

Shining Quotations:
https://amzn.in/d/9IkmdFP

Reflections of Wisdom:
https://amzn.in/d/2kQbqVx

WORLD FAMOUS QUOTATIONS:
https://amzn.in/d/cCXnGPR

INDIA A SPECTRUM OF HERITAGE:

MEMORABLE QUOTATION PART II :

Body, Mind & soul: Reflections of Mind

Enlightening Blissful Wisdom

ABOUT UPENDRA NATH RATH

International Writer • Poet • Story Writer • Educationist • Humanitarian

"Writing is not merely an art — it is a sacred duty to awaken values, kindle peace, and celebrate the divine in humanity.

Upendra Nath Rath

A Life Devoted to Knowledge and Service

Upendra Nath Rath stands as a beacon of literary brilliance and human compassion — a writer whose pen flows with wisdom, devotion, and the melody of truth.

Born in Odisha, India, he grew up amidst the serene landscapes that nurtured his love for nature, values, and humanity. His life journey — from a dedicated educator to an international author — reflects a harmonious blend of intellect, faith, and selfless service.

Academically distinguished, he holds multiple postgraduate degrees:

M.A. in English,

M.A. in Political Science,

M.A. in History,

MBA in Human Resources, and

B.Ed. in Education.

This rich academic background shaped his analytical mind and moral clarity, enabling him to weave knowledge with values in his teaching and writing alike.

Educational and Professional Journey

As a veteran educator under the Kendriya Vidyalaya Sangathan (KVS) Rath served across India — including Lumding (Assam),Waltair(A.P) Berhampur, Gopalpur INS Chilka, and Air Force StationSalua(Kolkata) .

His classrooms were more than academic spaces; they were sanctuaries of inspiration where he nurtured young minds with discipline, compassion, and creativity.

An ardent Scout and Guide Trainer, he earned the prestigious Himalayan Wood Badge (HWB), conducting numerous Scout camps and service programs. His leadership inspired thousands of students to embrace teamwork, environmental awareness, and moral living.

Literary and Creative Excellence

Upendra Nath Rath is the author of several acclaimed books, including:

Reflections of Wisdom

The Horizon of Values

Memorable Quotations

Enlightening Blissful Wisdom

Memorable Quotations for one and all

Shinning Quotation

Mind, Heart and Soul

His writings transcend boundaries of culture and geography — blending philosophy, ethics, and poetry with reflections on peace, nature, and education. His style is distinguished by clarity of thought, rhythmic prose, and universal humanism.

His quotations and reflections have inspired readers worldwide and are often described as "pearls of moral and intellectual illumination."

Social Service and Environmental Advocacy

A compassionate reformer, Rath has tirelessly organized social service camps for the poor, aged, and destitute in villages like Baxipalli, Golabandha, Digipur, and Berhampur.

His environmental initiatives — including massive plantation programs in Kendriya Vidyalayas — reflect his lifelong devotion to nature and sustainability.

Through these activities, he transformed education into action and compassion into community welfare.

Global Recognition and Awards

Received a Letter of Appreciation from the President of Switzerland (1998) for promoting World Peace.

Honored with the Incentive Award and Medal of Merit by the Deputy Commissioner, KVS (Bhubaneswar Region) for outstanding educational and social service.

Recognized internationally as a Brand Icon for Peace, Environmental Protection, and Value-Based Education.

Frequently invited to literary and cultural platforms for contributions to ethical writing, peace education, and moral leadership.

Vision and Philosophy

Rath's philosophy rests on the belief that education without values is incomplete and that literature must serve humanity.

His works emphasize harmony between mind, nature, and spirit, urging readers to discover inner potential and live with moral clarity.

He often says,

"The pen has the power to heal, unite, and awaken the soul of the world."

Personal Life and Legacy

Upendra Nath Rath continues to reside in Odisha, India, surrounded by books, birds, and nature his ever-inspiring companions.

When not writing, he spends his time guiding students, engaging in humanitarian efforts, and reflecting on universal truths.

His life remains a living example of discipline, simplicity, and devotion — a legacy of peace that will continue to inspire generations to come.

LIFE IN PICTURES

Staff Members memoirs at Kendriya Vidyalayas Waltair(Vishakha Patnam)

Shri Upendra Nath Rath leader of the Course is addressing the troop belonging to Rajya Puraskar.

Shri Upendra Nath Rath is receiving Medal of Merit award from Hon'ble Deputy Commissioner, BBSR.

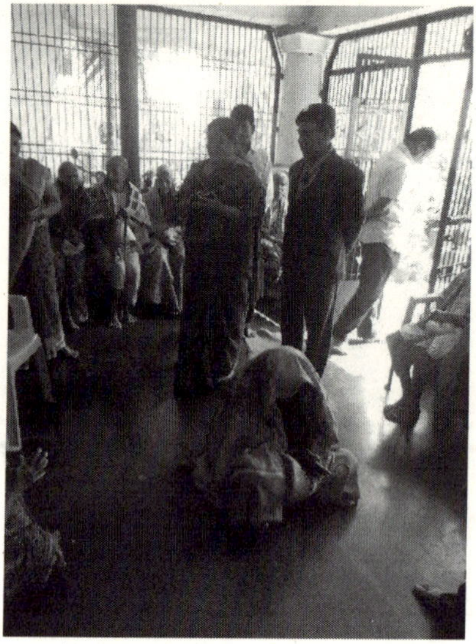

Joy of Giving camp is at Old age Home, Gopalpur on Sea.

Rastriya Ekta Diwas is being organized at Kendriya Vidyalayas Gopalpur Military Station by Upendra Nath Rath under the Guidance of Biraja Mishra Principal.

A joy of Giving program.is on progress in Berhampur.

Shri Upendra Nath Rath is addressing the teachers in English language in Central School, National Chatrapur.

A troop of emerging Scouters under the leadership of troop leadership of Sandip Sanam Rath

Scout Leader Upendra Nath Rath addressing the emerging Scouts of Rajya Puraskar.

KENDRIYA VIDYALAYA
MILITARY STATION

ASSOCIATE PARTNER
POSITIVE BARTA
AKASHVANI BHAVAN
PRASAR BHARATI, I & B MINISTRY
GOVT. OF INDIA, NEW DELHI
Visionary
Indians
Award
AWARDED BY
CELEBRITY GUEST
WE ARE PROUD TO ANNOUNCE
ESTEEMED AWARDEE
POONAM DHILLON
RENOWNED
BOLLYWOOD ACTRESS
18th
MAY
2025
UPENDRA NATH
RATH
EVENT BY
MEDIA PARTNER
MAGAZINE PARTNER
DIGITAL PARTNER
GOLDEN SPARROWS
GLOBAL ACHIEVERS
THINK A DIGITAL